Looking After Me

Taking Medicines

Written by Liz Gogerly
Illustrated by Mike Gordon

WAYLAND

I used to think medicine
was like magic.

A spoonful of syrup made a cough disappear.

Taaadaaa!!

A little bit of ointment made an itchy rash vanish.

A syringe of special pink liquid stopped a high temperature.

5

One day I thought
I'd try my magic out
on my old teddy, Jack.

I pretended I was a doctor
and he was my patient.

Lucikly for Jack there was a bottle of medicine on the counter. I was going to save his life!

But, still Jack
didn't look right.

So, I searched everywhere for more magic medicine.

I discovered some tablets next to mum's bed, and gave Jack five.

That's when Mum found us...
She was very angry!

She explained that I should never EVER play with medicines.

'Jimmy, tablets aren't sweets!'

I thought that medicines always made you better.

But they can make you ill if you take the wrong amount.

We need a doctor please.

Sometimes you should take your medicine after eating and other times you can't eat anything at all.

Mum made some new rules about medicines. All tablets, special mixtures and ointments were locked away.

Soon after the new rules, my dad had a cough and a sore throat.

Mum gave him some cough mixture and throat pastilles.

The pastilles soothed his throat
and soon he stopped coughing.

I caught Dad's cough.
Mum gave me some
cough mixture and
made me a hot
drink with lemon
and honey.

But, I still had a temperature and terrible earache so Mum took me to the doctor.

He said I had an ear infection and I needed antibiotics to make me better.

We took the prescription
to the pharmacy.

I needed three
spoons of the
medicine before food,
three times a day.

Mum put the medicine high up where I couldn't reach it.

After a few days my earache was gone!

Even though I felt better, it was important to finish all the antibiotics.

I know now that medicine is not really magic and there are different kinds of medicine, too.

My grandfather has tablets for his heart.

Jemima and Sally use inhalers because they have asthma.

Sometimes we have injections to protect us from illness or disease.

Special ointments can
help soothe a bee sting.

Antiseptic spray
kills germs in a
cut or graze.

Mum says you don't always need medicine to get better. Sometimes a good rest will make you feel tip top.

Eating healthy food and getting lots of exercise will keep you fit and strong.

NOTES FOR PARENTS AND TEACHERS

SUGGESTIONS FOR READING **LOOKING AFTER ME: TAKING MEDICINES** WITH CHILDREN

In this book we meet Jimmy, a young boy who learns that there's more to medicine than magic. At the start of the story he's playing with his teddy and manages to find some medicines. This would be a good time to talk to the children about what they think medicine does. Children often think that medicine will always make you better. The message of this book is that medicine can also be dangerous. Whether the medicine is an over-the-counter drug or on prescription it could still be a danger.

In the next section of the book Jimmy's parents introduce some house rules about medicine – simple rules that all caregivers should follow. Children will all have their own stories about where and how medicine is stored in their houses. It is important to stress that children should never tamper with bottles and try to open them. And, if they see pills in cardboard packages then they should leave them alone.

Some children may not understand the difference between prescription and non-prescription medicines. When Jimmy's father falls ill he uses over-the-counter drugs. However, when Jimmy is ill he needs stronger medicine that can fight his ear infection. Jimmy's experience introduces children to how we get prescription medicines. Children may already know this process and you can encourage them to talk about their own experiences. The story also aims to show that some medicines are necessary for saving people's lives. Jimmy's grandfather needs medication for his heart and his friends need an inhaler for their asthma. Perhaps the children can think of other drugs or medicines that people take to save their lives.

The book ends on a high note. Medicines are there to help us, and, if they are used correctly, they usually do make us better. However, our bodies are also amazing healing machines and as well as taking medicines we can help keep ourselves healthy by eating well and keeping fit.

LOOKING AFTER ME AND THE NATIONAL CURRICULUM

The Looking After Me series of books is aimed at children studying PSHE at Key Stage 1. In the section *Knowledge, skills and understanding: Developing a healthy, safer lifestyle pupils* of the National Curriculum, it is stated that pupils are expected to 'learn about themselves as developing individuals and as members of their communities, building on their own experiences and on the early learning goals for personal, social and emotional development'.

Children are expected to learn:
• how to make simple choices that improve their health and well-being to maintain personal hygiene;
• how some diseases spread and can be controlled;
• about the process of growing from young to old and how people's needs change;
• the names of the main parts of the body;
• that all household products, including medicines, can be harmful if not used properly;
• rules for, and ways of, keeping safe, including basic road safety, and about people who can help them to stay safe.

BOOKS TO READ

First Look At: Do I have to go to hospital Pat Thomas
(Wayland 2008)
Helping Hands: In the doctor's surgery Ruth Thomson
(Wayland 2006)
The Big Day: Going to Hospital Nicola Barber (Wayland 2008)

ACTIVITY:

Present children with a selection of packaging for medicines —
for example tablets, solutions — and ask them to decide how
they know that they are not packaging for food or sweets.
Then, together with the children, make a collage or
display to illustrate packaging for medicines and
how they help medicines to be used safely.
Talk with children about the use of medicines
and when we may need them.

INDEX

32